Rocks, Rocks, Rocks

by Mickey Daronco and Diane Ohanesian

I can have a rock
for my neck.

Rick can have
a rock for luck.

Can I tuck a rock
in my red sock?

Jack can pick a big rock for a pet.

Can the rock be a puck?

Vick can pick
a rock to kick.

We all can have fun
on the big, big rock!